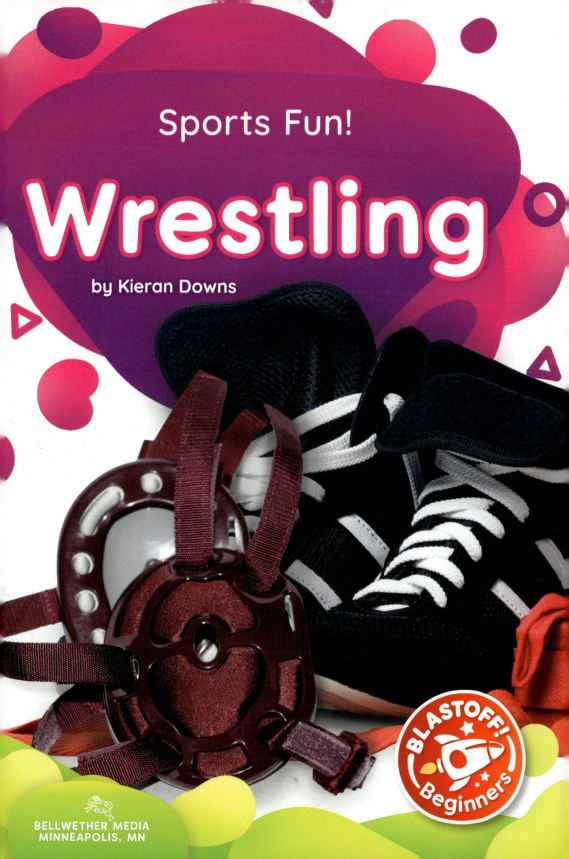

Sports Fun!
Wrestling

by Kieran Downs

BELLWETHER MEDIA • MINNEAPOLIS, MN

Blastoff! Beginners are developed by literacy experts and educators to meet the needs of early readers. These engaging informational texts support young children as they begin reading about their world. Through simple language and high frequency words paired with crisp, colorful photos, Blastoff! Beginners launch young readers into the universe of independent reading.

Sight Words in This Book

a	go	on	this
are	he	one	time
can	in	other	to
down	is	people	with
for	it	the	
get	make	they	

This edition first published in 2024 by Bellwether Media, Inc.

No part of this publication may be reproduced in whole or in part without written permission of the publisher. For information regarding permission, write to Bellwether Media, Inc., Attention: Permissions Department, 6012 Blue Circle Drive, Minnetonka, MN 55343.

Library of Congress Cataloging-in-Publication Data

Names: Downs, Kieran, author.
Title: Wrestling / by Kieran Downs.
Description: Minneapolis, MN : Bellwether Media, Inc., 2024. | Series: Blastoff! Beginners: Sports fun! | Includes bibliographical references and index. | Audience: Ages 4-7 | Audience: Grades K-1
Identifiers: LCCN 2023004978 (print) | LCCN 2023004979 (ebook) | ISBN 9798886873979 (library binding) | ISBN 9798886875850 (ebook)
Subjects: LCSH: Wrestling--Juvenile literature.
Classification: LCC GV1195.3 .D72 2024 (print) | LCC GV1195.3 (ebook) | DDC 796.812--dc23/eng/20230201
LC record available at https://lccn.loc.gov/2023004978
LC ebook record available at https://lccn.loc.gov/2023004979

Text copyright © 2024 by Bellwether Media, Inc. BLASTOFF! BEGINNERS and associated logos are trademarks and/or registered trademarks of Bellwether Media, Inc.

Editor: Rebecca Sabelko   Designer: Jeffrey Kollock

Printed in the United States of America, North Mankato, MN.

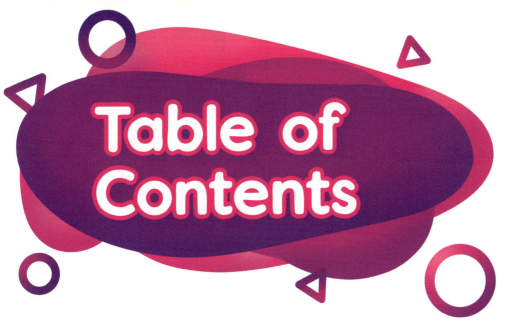

Table of Contents

Time to Wrestle!	4
What Is Wrestling?	6
On the Mat	14
Wrestling Facts	22
Glossary	23
To Learn More	24
Index	24

Time to Wrestle!

Wrestlers get on the **mat**. It is time to wrestle!

What Is Wrestling?

People wrestle in **matches**. They face off on a mat.

People face off one-on-one. They are also on a team.

They get points for moves. The most points wins.

They can also win with a **pin**!

On the Mat

Wrestlers wear tight clothes.

They go for **takedowns.**

One wrestler holds the other down. Point!

This wrestler makes a pin. He wins the match!

Wrestling Facts

Wrestling

tight clothes

mat

Wrestling Moves

pin

takedown

hold wrestlers down

Glossary

mat

a place where wrestling matches happen

matches

times when two people or teams wrestle

pin

a winning move in a wrestling match

takedowns

moves used to bring another wrestler down to the mat

To Learn More

ON THE WEB

FACTSURFER

Factsurfer.com gives you a safe, fun way to find more information.

1. Go to www.factsurfer.com.

2. Enter "wrestling" into the search box and click 🔍.

3. Select your book cover to see a list of related content.

Index

clothes, 14
face off, 6, 8
holds, 18
mat, 4, 5, 6
matches, 6, 20
moves, 10
one-on-one, 8
pin, 12, 20
points, 10, 18

takedowns, 16, 17
team, 8
wins, 10, 12, 20
wrestlers, 4, 14, 18, 20

The images in this book are reproduced through the courtesy of: Nicholas Piccillo, front cover; Aleksey Kurguzov, front cover, p. 3; Marko Aliaksandr, p. 3; Perry Correll, p. 4; Ahturner, pp. 5, 22 (wrestling); A_Lesik, pp. 7, 19, 22 (pin), 23 (takedowns); Peter Muzslay, p. 9; Susan Leggett, p. 11; Jeremy Polanski/ Flickr, pp. 13, 22 (takedown, hold); Everyonephoto Studio, pp. 15, 17, 21, 23 (pin); Ralf Geithe, p. 23 (mat); Adil Celebiyev StokPhoto, p. 23 (matches).